Old Scooter Poetry

(not too poetic)

poems by

Karen Lee

Finishing Line Press
Georgetown, Kentucky

Old Scooter Poetry

(not too poetic)

Copyright © 2025 by Karen Lee
ISBN 979-8-89990-095-2 First Edition
All rights reserved under International and Pan-American Copyright Conventions.
No part of this book may be reproduced in any manner whatsoever without written permission from the publisher, except in the case of brief quotations embodied in critical articles and reviews.

Publisher: Leah Huete de Maines
Editor: Christen Kincaid
Cover Art by Karen Lee klee6@hotmail.com
All other images: Donnie Reed dreedmba@gmail.com
Cover Design: Elizabeth Maines McCleavy

Order online: www.finishinglinepress.com
also available on amazon.com

Author inquiries and mail orders:
Finishing Line Press
PO Box 1626
Georgetown, Kentucky 40324
USA

Contents

Old Scooter Prologue 1

Old Scooter Origins 2

Old Scooters Death 4

Old Scooter Magic 5

Old Scooter Shadow Rider 7

Old Scooter Breakdown I 8

Old Scooter Breakdown II 9

The Old Scooter She 10

Old Scooter Romance I 12

Old Scooter Romance II 13

Old Scooter Song I 14

Old Scooter Song II 15

Old Scooter Sidecar 16

Old Scooter Anger 18

Old Scooter Blind Spot 19

Old Scooter Epilogue 20

*This book of poetry is dedicated to my husband Jeff,
who is forever collecting old scooters and worrying about
what will happen to them when they both die.*

Old Scooter Prologue

A single spar that ran from the headstock to the rear.

A U shape,
leaving space for legs.

Front and rear wheels, were interchangeable.

A Roman Holiday,
Peck and Hepburn.
A symbol of freedom and imagination.

Bolbous rear,
slim waist,
antenna-like handlebars.

Paris Dakar Rally,
The 400 covered with a car.

The Motherly, The Siluro, for the future
The Alpha, for secret agents,
The Giant, for artists.

The Troupes Aero Portees,
T. A. P.
equipped with a 75mm M20,
penetrated 100mm of steel armour.

"Sembra una vespa", looks like wasp.

A legend was born.

Old Scooter Origins

Four stroke or
two stroke, oil in the gas.

Put it away for winter
no riding in the snow.

Skinny tires for balance.
Keep the handlebars aligned.

Can't find the
vin. Can't get the title.

Made in Italy the only
thing we know.

Patina just a
fancy name for rust.

Parts are unavailable,
have to make your own.

Main goal: keep it
running, forever.

Drive it across the country,
just to prove it can.

Like an old lover not much
spark left. Tickle it every
now and then, to make sure
it will still go.

Old Scooters Death

Parts piled everywhere
old scooter cemetery
a sense of mourning
about the place, the smell
of death.

Disassembled, broken,
apart, some pieces
cataloged some
discarded, simply too
damaged to recreate.

Like the valve of
a human heart,
a smoker, an oil fiend,
a clean engine
with power still to offer?

However, there's a sense of
renewal, where parts will be
remade into another,
creating time for
a future ride.

Old Scooter Magic

Sit upon the
seat of any
forty-year-old scooter,
wait for the magic.

It will appear,
like a vibration,
a fabrication,
a persuasion.

Fire it up,
experience moments of its
life, listen for the story,
it eagerly recites.

Roll it down the road,
feel the power it still
commands, as it begs
 to keep its wheels
spinning into the echo of its ride.

Old Scooter Shadow Rider

Every biker knows
the shadow rider,
he follows along
on a sun filled day
gliding across
the pavement.

He moves in and out
as he's obstructed by
buildings, trees and clouds,
but nonetheless to
follows the path of the
riders.

He might grow larger or
smaller as he comes into view,
he might grow dimmer or
brighter as the day
wears on and the
path grows narrow.

Bikers take pictures of
him, that never seem to
develop, like a
ghost rider wandering in and
out of their view,
in and out of the ride.

He is always there to
entertain, follow the
path, take notice,
create a reflection of
the moment at hand,
never lost.

Old Scooter Breakdown I

We are so far out
we don't even
know where.

Little reception, low battery,
Who to call?
Where to go?

Push it, curse at it
kick it, choke it
open the case apply a wrench.

Spray starter fluid,
talk to it,
give it a rest.

Can't leave it
behind, can't
vamoose.

How long will we
sit here,
only the scooter knows.

We have water,
we have snacks,
we'll last for hours, I'm told.

Sitting on the curb
a soft breeze in my hair,
shiny sky, no rain.

The beautiful woods behind
me is alive,
I hear movement?!

Old Scooter Breakdown II

We push her into the scenic overlook
a group of people spy us.
As usual the men wonder over to help
they pick up tools, give advice.

I take off my helmet,
shake out my hair.
As usual the women turn their backs,
I hear "rider" in their heads.

I turn, look out at the overlook,
a moment, a catch in my breath.
A sea of trees before me,
green and red, golden and orange.

The sounds of leaves softly falling,
blanketing the earth.
I look back at her,
she looks tired.

The men gather around her
like surgeons dissecting her parts.
A hope that she will,
make it through another day.

I turn back to the trees,
this is why we rolled her out from the dark corner of the garage.
So, she could feel the wind on her frame
hear the click, click of the gravel on an old country road.

Together we smell the leaves,
she and I.
As the trees prepare
for another winter solstice.
And possibly
our last ride.

The Old Scooter She

At first I hated the She,
the macho ownership,
of another female.

But then I rode,
traveled,
traversed across the land.

After a while
I began to agree,
only She could glide,
as gracefully, poised and compassionate.

The steadiness
that She maneuvers on her wheels,
the power of her skeletal frame.

The endurance
of her motor's velocity,
the journey as She provides life's passage.

I see the She,
that captivates the power,
that lures the riders,
to the road.

Old Scooter Romance I

Wheels, wheels, helmet, seat
boy on the front
girl on the back
a slow ride down a narrow street
shocks on front
cobblestones bouncing the pillion seat
clutching his waist
making sure not to lean
time to be with him
even when it feels like
she's falling off.

Old Scooter Romance II

I leaned my body
across his back.

Maybe I had one too
many gin and tonics.

I believe I am safe as
the wind blows my hair across my back.

He knows me,
when I've had too many.

Years and years,
and years and years,
leaning on his back,
safely riding home.

As age has replaced,
fast cars, fast dancing,
loud bands,
warm erotic night.

Slow drifting by the moonlight,
on an old scooter is all
it takes to find
romance.

Old Scooter Song I
(Subtitle: Me watching you start an Old Scooter)

heavy boot
rider's jacket
helmet

heel to starter
slam down
nothing

heel to starter
choke
slam down
sputter, sputter, die

heel to starter
slam down
sputter, sputter, sputter
die

"NOOOOO"

off the bike
take a break
shake out heavy boot
take off helmet

heel to starter
slam down
"too old for this shit"

deep breath
heal to starter
choke
slam down
sputter, sputter, varoom

shove on helmet
yell at me
"get the hell on"

Old Scooter Song II

Since '46 they heard
the call, come ride me,
come ride me.

I'll find you a happy
road, with flowering trees, and
fields of poppies.

I'll carry you through the
green forests the
dry desert, the
steep mountains.

I'll carry you through the
warm sunshine, the
drizzly rain, the
soft moonlight.

Come ride me, come
ride me,
down a winding road.

Come ride me, come
ride me,
on an open beach.

Since '46 they heard
the call and we had them
when we named her Vespa.

Old Scooter Sidecar

Definition
a car attached to the side of a scooter for a passenger
a cocktail consisting of a liqueur with lemon juice and brandy

Sometimes known a place for…
the dog,
the grandkids,
extra parts dragged home.

In racing the
passenger
balancing
the ride, known as the
sidecar monkey.

In old movies,
comes apart
dumping the
passenger
in the lake.

In WWI used to
convey the good
Captain for its
name's sake
cocktail.

Nowadays it's
where I sit
watching for lakes
and sipping my Sidecar.

Old Scooter Anger
(Subtitle: Read me with an old scooter accent)

I like to spin down the street, rider on my back. The thump, thump sound of my wheels, the bounce of my shocks, the rev of my engine as we roll, roll, roll.

I love ridden in traffic, feeling the movement all around me.

Until some hog pulls up next to me. They always seem to snort, a little macho laugh like I'm teenager out for a ride. "I'm three times your age asshole and I've got more time on these gears than you've been alive." I shout back, but they're so loud they can't hear me. They rev their engine and pull through the light before I have time to even twist shift my gears.

Other times it's a jacked-up Honda with its dual exhaust. They don't so much snort as they snicker on by. I nudge my rider to kick their doors. I don't need no smack talk, no hip-hop blasting from your car. They tailgate me as if they need to push me along, I'm goin the speed limit.

Sometimes I get a young woman in van with four kids. The kids love me, they point and smile. But not her. She's in such a hurry she passes me on the right, cuttin' me off trying to get around me.

And don't get me started on stop signs and stop lights. Cars turn in front of me before I make it into the intersection.

Someday soon I'm gonna lose it. I gonna do a donut in the middle of the street. Stop the traffic from all four sides. Roar my engine and blow my pipes and shout, "Look out assholes, I'm coming through."

If only I could talk.

Old Scooter Blind Spot

Like the sock lost in the dryer.
Like the key that lost its lock.
Like the lid to a storage container nowhere to be found,

And so, it is for the old scooter right mirror.

No easy way to see behind,
no lane changes to the right.

A struggling ride that reveals the past,
only to be seen on the left.

An authentic replacement,
hard to find,
suffer the repop, knock off.

Somewhere there is a world,
with a pile of single socks,
a ring of keys to nothing,
a lid that won't be sealed,
only seen in a scooter
rear-view mirror,
on the right side.

Old Scooter Epilogue

Sometimes a barn
find, rusted beyond
repair, all patina
no wheels, no motor.

Sometimes used as
backyard planter,
sign display, broken
pieces for another.

Often torn apart,
seat cut off for
sale, side cowls
become hearts of art.

Fallen on its
side, covered
by dirt, pieces
for a scrap yard.

Its time on the
road over,
decayed beyond
repair.

Always a sad
memory of what it
was, of how
it ran the road.

Picture the rider,
lean in, listen for the
rev, the click, click
the wind's hum.

It's like lost
music from the
past, rarely seen
or heard again.

Karen Lee is an avid poet, fiction writer, playwright, and graphic artist, and photographer. She resides in Cicero, Indiana but travels the world for fun. This is her first full length poetry chapbook. *Old Scooter Poetry* is written as a tribute to her husband Jeff and his constant hording of old vespa scooters, parts, and books. She is not an enthusiastic scooter driver but an experience rider. She has enjoyed many scooter rides, breakdowns and rallies. She is a member of the VCOA. Recently she attended the Vespa World Conference in Pontederia, Italy. Karen Lee writes poetry that falls out of her head onto the page. She writes middle grade fiction that uplifts normal girls that don't kick ass. She writes cathartic life essays with her tongue in her cheek. When she's not doing all that, she teaches graphic designs while continuously creating her own art. She is a constant and perpetual student herself taking class from Stanford University, Gotham Writers Workshops and the local writer center here in Indianapolis. Her goal: hone her skills so it shows in every work she creates.

www.ingramcontent.com/pod-product-compliance
Lightning Source LLC
Chambersburg PA
CBHW022107080426
42734CB00009B/1502